MW00437416

Freedom's Dance

SARA VEVANG

Foreword by: Lorisa Miller

LUCIDBOOKS

Freedom's Dance

Copyright © 2019 by Sara Vevang

Artwork by Lindsey Colwill

Published by Lucid Books in Houston, TX
www.LucidBooksPublishing.com

All rights reserved. No part of this publication may be reproduced, stored in a retrieval system, or transmitted in any form by any means, electronic, mechanical, photocopy, recording, or otherwise, without the prior permission of the publisher, except as provided for by USA copyright law.

hardback ISBN-10: 1-63296-289-6
hardback ISBN-13: 978-1-63296-289-8
eISBN-10: 1-63296-284-5
eISBN-13: 978-1-63296-284-3

Scripture quotations are taken from the Holy Bible, New International Version®, NIV®. Copyright © 1973, 1978, 1984, 2011 by Biblica, Inc.™ Used by permission of Zondervan. All rights reserved worldwide. www.zondervan.com The "NIV" and "New International Version" are trademarks registered in the United States Patent and Trademark Office by Biblica, Inc.™

Special Sales: Most Lucid Books titles are available in special quantity discounts. Custom imprinting or excerpting can also be done to fit special needs. Contact Lucid Books at Info@LucidBooksPublishing.com.

Table of Contents

Special Thanks

Terry K. Lindsey
November 15, 1959–August 20, 2018
He loved without limits. He told me I was eloquent and I have a voice. He made me feel safe. I am so grateful to have known him.

Sharla Brenneman
Who showed me the way, when I knew no other. Taking time out of her busy schedule to teach me and comfort me. I'm forever changed!

Briana McIntyre
A fearless woman who calls out the best in people.
She told me I was a writer. Thank you!

Naci Littlejohn
She gave me my journal as a gift and encouraged me to write. She said it would be a book one day. She was right. Thanks for loving me so well.

My husband, Eric
Who supports me and refuses to let me be mediocre. My precious daughters, Vera, Scarlett, and Abigail. The most amazing family I could ask for. Thank you, Jesus, for my friends and family!

Foreword

Jesus heals things: broken bones, broken relationships, broken hearts, and shattered souls. He sets captives free. He said it Himself when He stood up in the temple and read Isaiah 61 aloud. Freedom is a high value for our Lord. In fact, the Bible says that "it is for freedom that Christ has set us free" (Gal. 5:1).

He's not afraid of our mess and our vulnerability. In fact, when we bring our weaknesses to Him, He takes delight in them. We have a lot to learn from Him in this regard. Most of us shy away from messy, raw honesty. We squirm in our seats when someone bares the deepest parts of their soul. But not Jesus. It's in that space of mess that He does His best work. You see, it's in our weakness that He shows Himself strong. It's a broken and contrite spirit to which He is drawn. He delights in showing mercy. He draws near to the broken-hearted. It's in that space where we can smell His fragrance.

And this is the space that Sara has courageously invited us into—the space where heaven touches earth and a perfect Healer touches a broken heart. As I read her poems, I am drawn into that space with her. I can sense my own brokenness being overshadowed by the hope of His nearness, His voice, His healing balm, His words of life.

This space is beautifully raw and you may find yourself squirming in your seat as you read her honest words. And if you do, welcome Him into your discomfort. Allow the fragrance of her worship to overwhelm you as it does Him. Remember how the Pharisees squirmed as Mary Magdalene poured out her dignity and brokenness in an act of worship? But not Jesus. He didn't squirm. He received her and took great delight in her. He said she would be known everywhere the gospel is preached. In a similar fashion, Sara pours out the oil of her heart onto her Savior. May you find your voice in Sara's, as she reaches out in hope and faith to invite the Lover of her soul to shed His light into every dark place.

Unto Him be all glory,
Lorisa Miller
Senior Leader
UPPERROOM

I Live

I live in an ocean with a straw
I live here this is where I live
This is all I know
An ocean with a straw
I'm tossed by the waves with my straw
I'm beaten and I'm tattered with my straw
I choke and I gasp with my straw
I fight for life with my straw
I scream and I cry with my straw
Occasionally I just want to die with my straw
It's like I can't breathe at all
Where is the man that walks on water
To save me from my life with the straw
To pull me in from the undertow
To change my world and all I know
This can't be how life is supposed to go
I just can't breathe unless I let you go
I want to live a life without the straw
I want to live and breathe it all
I want to thrive up somewhere higher
Than these crashing waves that make me tired
Where is my lifeboat please pull me in
I want to live and be who I am within

Come Out

Why do we have the good and the bad
Why do girls spend a lifetime without a dad
Will he ever care will he ever want to know
Who I am or how my children have grown

It seems to me I can't escape it
Either let your heart break or try and fake it
To grieve is to feel and to feel is to know
The pain is so deep
Why don't the tears flow

I'm terrified if I start I will never stop
The numb sensation in my heart, let it open
I want to be done with this
Come out come out wherever you're hiding
It's safe to come and stay

How will I live without you healed
With this hurting inside I just can't feel
I can't live with this pain inside
It makes me want to close up and hide
From those around me

They need me they are just babies
They need me healthy
They need me free
Think of what you will miss
I want to be done with this
Oh tears come out

Permission to Feel

You cannot feel unless you heal
you cannot heal unless you feel
world stop and just stay still

To love is to live and
to live is to die
please take a moment
to just sit and
cry

You say you have bottles
that catch all my tears
they float like messages
in rivers of love that drown out
all my fears

As they flow out
Your perfect love rushes in
it fills all the places
where hatred has been

May I Have This Dance

Spirit of my heart
Awake oh sleepy soul
Be new Be new
Be what God called you to do
If you don't believe you can be set free
Come and dance with Me and I will set you free
Awake Awake
Awake my sleepy soul
There is no pain no more
Arise Arise
For you have been set free
Arise Arise
Come and dance with Me
Spirit of my heart come and take what's Yours
Spirit of my heart
Here's what You're looking for
Awake Awake
Awake my weakened soul
You have been made new
For Jesus told me so
Believe Believe
Come and dance
with Me

Who Can This Be

This man that doesn't leave
He cares for me so deeply
His love is always mine
He's like a sunken treasure
That everyone can find

This chest it never closes
His heart is open wide
It's like He stands there shouting
Please come and look inside
My lock it never latches
My hinges never rust
The only thing it takes to open
Is trust

Distracted by Your Love

Your love is not fleeting
He set it before us for all to find
Into Your throne room I run
In spirit and truth
You lead me You guide me
He holds my hand and walks beside me
You burn away a soul dividing
You turn my world upside down
And now it's thriving
Distracted by You I just can't
Look at me
I see Your face and choose Your
GLORY

Frustrated with Me

What I know is true
I don't believe
Frustrated with me
Every day I could have done better
Frustrated with me
I should have, I could have, I didn't, I don't
Stop it but I won't
No one is perfect so how can I be
I want so badly to love myself
And then there's me

I Am Disappointment

Hide me
Keep me locked away
Throw away the key
Pretend I don't bother you
Pretend I don't lead you astray
Pretend I don't exist
Maybe I will just disappear
Maybe it will fix itself
Is it even real
Is it my fault
What did I do
Will this ever end
Keep your hand in your pocket
Shouts the mind of the man
With the withered hand
Don't reveal me
They won't understand

Disconnected and Deceived

Life isn't anything I thought it would be
It's the hardest that it ever could be
In the same room but miles apart
When you say I love you
It does nothing to my heart
We literally live on two different planets
Lonely and suffocated all at the same time
Is this life really mine
How does it end and how does it begin
Responsible for you is making me crazy
Don't you see I have enough babies
This constant I'm sorry, I shouldn't have said that
I put a guard up as soon as you open your mouth
Judging others instead of learning
I guess you're too smart to listen
I just don't know if I have this in me
Being around you is a constant responsibility
I'm not sure why I'm here anymore
Operating around you is like a raging war
Inside my mind
We have hardly anything in common
You coming towards me makes me want to reverse
I can recall every curse
Make the choice not to rehearse
It's all in my head everything you've said
Years of death spoken over me
Now I'm just supposed to be happy
It's impossible
But Jesus right?
He gave His life
So I choose to give mine
You're killing me in the process
Of trying to die

I Trust You Jesus

I give You my whole heart
I trust You Jesus
I give You my whole life
I trust You Jesus
I give You my identity
I trust You Jesus
I give You my future
I trust You Jesus
I give You my emotions
I trust You Jesus
I give You my marriage
I trust You Jesus
I give You my family
I trust You Jesus
For the joy set before me
I trust You Jesus

Liar

You lied to me
You promised me the world
And all you did was take it
You promised me a life full of love
And all you did was break it
How could you have done this
Why didn't I know
It's like a beautiful garden
That was never allowed to grow
Now you stand before me
Asking for a second chance
Saying it as easy as may I have this dance
A dance of death or is it life
God only knows but
I choose to try

Sacrifice to You My King

Let my praises rise to the heavenlies
Let my praises rise to the
King of kings
In my trials and in my pain
My sacrifice will rise
To the One who has
Changed my life and called me
His bride
I will forever cry worthy to
My King
No matter what my life will bring
Through my trials
And through my pain
I will bring You my sacrifice of
praise

My Father

Under Your wings is where I hide
Under Your wings is where I thrive
Your safety draws me back
Again and again
It calls to me when life grabs and bends
In Your shadows is where I stay
You take care of me and never cause me to stray
It's You who sets me free
It's You who takes the lead
The greatest gentlemen I see is willing to live inside of me
To die for me
To cry for me
To pierce His hands and cut His side for me
To rise for me
To open heaven's gates wide for me
To cause this spirit to
Come alive in me
This is who my Father is
And always will be

Beauty

My beauty is a gift and a blessing
It is not a curse or a weapon
Every flower, every tree, every planet, every thing
Points to my King
We are made in His image
From Creator to creation
My God gives me the power to take the nations
A woman of influence is what He calls me
He gave me this face
He gave me these dreams
I'm not an object or less than
I'm a beautiful woman and here I stand
Every time you objectify me it pushes me further
To my purpose and to my Father
He says this is my daughter
In whom I am well-pleased
He will never hurt or objectify me
Object no longer
I am not your slave
Jesus Christ handled that when
He went to the grave

Expectations

Why don't empty tea bags bring forth tea
Can a man walk without any knees
Can a woman cry if she doesn't have eyes
Do bees make honey if they don't have a hive
Why don't you see all that's going on with me
You cannot get out what isn't there
Empty just doesn't produce
Freedom isn't free when you're wearing a noose

Can you take a bath in a tub with no water
It takes most of me to care for my daughters
I give what I have and it's never enough
This isn't a cake walk
It's extremely tough
Who are you to tell me
What you need
You suffocate me so much
I can hardly breathe
When will this end
When will you know
You are only hurting us
And stunting any growth

Me

I hear You say I am fearfully
And wonderfully made
Why can't I see it
Everything in the world around me
Screams you're not good enough
How come I believe it
Days go by so up and down
It's like I'm on a roller coaster
With no solid ground
If I could see who You made me to be
Somehow I'd find myself and
Finally be free

Your Love

Your love is like a summer wave
A winter's cool crisp breeze
It makes me laugh
It makes me cry
It brings me to my knees
Your love amazes me
Drives me to peace
Renews my mind again and again
My worship is extravagant when I look at You
No matter what my life brings
It's all I live to do

Into Me You See

Where is the passion in lovemaking
Yes it's a risk and worth taking
There is more in connection than connecting
Why is this issue so extremely pressing
I will not be threatened into this
It is my life and I'll choose my risk
I'm hurt I was reduced to a screen
Objectified I won't be
It's extremely mean
As days go by I keep getting stronger
Learning of love and I'm not going to settle
Don't try and convince me it's always my fault
You keep your lies locked in a vault
The truth comes out
Like it or not
His light shines on every dark place
I will not be tricked
I won't be lied to
I will not live in this deadly cycle
Love will be love and sex will be sex
I'm not an object on anyone's shelf
Intimacy is how we connect

Anger

Anger you are destroying me
You cause me to be blinded by my feelings
Anger you are my worst enemy
No longer can you captivate me
Bringing me to miss the simple things
Blocking me from the enjoyment of life
Living in anger and strife
Angry you are ruling my days
Trying to make me live in a haze
Anger you can't make me that way anymore
I'm changing my mind and shutting those doors
Pack up your memories
Pack up your hurt
Hand them over to the One who loved you first

Prepare to be BIG

I look forward to today
I awake with expectation
I do not feel threatened or in the way
I was made for a purpose
My life has a cause
I am a teacher
I am a fighter
She has a world of wealth and
Knowledge inside her

Unhindered

I am hindered by nothing
I am hindered by no one
I laugh in the face of opposition
It won't force me to change my position
I've got plans and I've got dreams
Don't even think you can steal them
With your evil schemes
Made for a purpose
I'm made by design
Up in heaven I've got a blueprint
That's only mine
You think you can steal it
You thought you could edit
I've got news for you Satan
You're not in my credits

Numb

Immovable unshakeable
In the worst way
This numb feeling in my mind
Tries to make me feel the same
Numb you can't stay here
I won't let you get in my way
I've got a life to live
Numb isn't welcome here
I'll move I'll shake
I will awake
No matter what it takes
Numb you just can't stay

Alive

I am alive
I am alive
Because my Savior died
He died for me
Up on that tree
And now I live in victory
I am alive
I am alive
Because my Savior died
No longer slaves
To anything
We're alive
We're alive
In
Victory

Resting Face

If a smile were my resting face
The world would be a happier place
My face would be exciting
And my world would be inviting
Children would feel accepted
Adults wouldn't feel rejected
Just smile for goodness' sake

You Take Pleasure in My Every Prayer

We are never separated
You vindicate me as I walk in all integrity
Redeeming me in Your gracious love
Purity is what You seek
Refining fire burns darkness out of me
Your blood You shed on Calvary
Paid the price
Now I'm forever
In communion with
My Jesus Christ

Frozen

Frozen has a choice to melt
Melting isn't easy
Melting isn't fun
Melting gets messy
The pain burns as it runs
Memories turn from color
To bloodstained red
You paid a high price for me not to be frozen
For me to enjoy life and not be numb

When I Grow Up

I will be a great mother
I will forgive all the memories
Being hurt by others
I will be honored and
Cherished and loved
Knowing my true Father is
Smiling from above
I will teach of all that I have learned
Never being afraid
Of each page as it turns

You Do

I made you
I made your brain
You do have opinions
You do have thoughts
I made you wonderful
I made you kind
You do love people
You have a great smile
I made you for My glory
I made you My divine
You do have a purpose
You do have time
You do have a voice

The Fullness of Empty

You walked out of the grave for me
So I will dance with You
You captured sin and death for me
So I know what I choose
I bring You my offering
I pour it out on you
My life is the most costly thing
I give it all to you
Enjoy the life I gave to you or I died in vain
I redeemed you on the cross that day
I took away your guilt and shame
I died for you so you could thrive
Up somewhere higher than these chasing waves that make you tired
I saved you from the eternal fire
My name be lifted higher
Above the storm
Above the waves
I choose the dance of life
Thank You for the empty grave

Finally Free

It's foreign being me
This girl that I see
Is nothing like she used to be
She is fierce
She is free
She's becoming who she's made to be
This process like a bouncy ball
Sometimes you stand sometimes you fall
Our weakness made perfect in His strength
So we can dance another day
From captive to captivated
Freedom is so liberating
The taste of full no longer empty
Washed in blood now sparkling
Mirror you no longer lie to me
Beaming walking from glory to glory
Communing with the King of kings
You set a table in the presence of my enemies
Your daughter is finally free

About the Illustrator

Lindsey Colwill, an amazing illustrator, was born and bred in Texas, graduating from the University of North Texas with a BFA in Art Education. She used this experience to teach elementary school art for 10 years. As a wife and mother of two, she then chose to nurture her greatest creations, her kids, full-time. Lindsey has enjoyed the beauty of dance her whole life and relishes combining it with her artistry. Her heart is to display the beauty of God's creation.

About the Body Study

Brecca McIntyre, our body study, has been dancing for 17 years. God has given her a heart that loves all things creative—not only dance, but art in all forms for the purposes of worship and glorifying His name. She was given the opportunity to dance for the illustrator to bring visuals alive in this book.

CPSIA information can be obtained
at www.ICGtesting.com
Printed in the USA
BVHW092238080119
537354BV00001B/4/P

9 781632 962898